KINGFISHER
a Houghton Mifflin Company imprint
222 Berkeley Street
Boston, Massachusetts 02116
www.houghtonmifflinbooks.com

First published in 2004
2 4 6 8 10 9 7 5 3

LIBRARY OF CONGRESS CATALOGING–IN–PUBLICATION DATA
Seriously silly school jokes/illustrated by Tony Trimmer
p. cm.—Sidesplitters
ISBN 0-7534-5725-3
1. Schools—Juvenile humor. 2. Education—Juvenile humor.
3. Wit and humor, Juvenile. I. Trimmer, Tony. II. Series.
PN6231.S3S47 2005
818'.60208—dc22   2004007897

ISBN 0-7534-5725-3
ISNBN 978-07534-5725-2

Printed in India
2TR/1104/THOM/FR/90INDWF/F

Seriously Silly School Jokes

Illustrated by **Tony Trimmer**

KINGFISHER
BOSTON

Teacher: Johnny, have you given the fish in the aquarium any fresh water?
Johnny: No, they haven't drunk this water yet.

Teacher: If you had $2 in one pocket and $4 in the other, what would you have altogether, Tom?
Tom: Someone else's jeans.

Teacher: You're late. You should have been here at 9 o'clock.
Student: Why? Did something happen?

Teacher: Give me three collective nouns.
Student: Garbage can, vacuum cleaner, and dustpan.

Teacher: Can anyone tell me where elephants can be found?
Student: Don't be silly, they're much too big to lose.

Alexis: Dad, can you write in the dark?
Dad: Sure I can. What do you want me to write?
Alexis: Your name on my report card.

Why did the teacher send Dracula's son home?
Because he was "coffin" so much.

What did the ghost teacher say to her students?
"Now look at the board while I go through it again."

Teacher: What's the difference between an Indian elephant and an African elephant?

Student: Around 3,000 miles.

How do teachers dress in the winter?

Quickly.

What's the difference between a teacher and a train?
One says, "Spit out that bubble gum," and the other says, "Choo choo!"

What stands in the middle of Paris?
The letter "r."

David went to the school cafeteria and bought a juice box at lunchtime. He hadn't finished all of it before he went into his geography class, so he stuffed it in his pocket. The teacher asked the class,

"What do we call people living in China?"

"Chinese."

"What do we call people living in America?"

"American."

"Now, David, since all you seem to be doing is fooling around with whatever's in your pocket can you tell me what we call people living in Europe?"

"Er, no . . ."

"European," shouted a voice from the back of the classroom.

"No, I'm not," said David. "My juice box is leaking."

Justin: I'm sorry I'm late for school, but I was having a dream about basketball.
Teacher: Why does having a dream about basketball make you late for school?
Justin: They played extra time.

How can a teacher double her money?
By folding it in half.

Teacher: Why were the Pilgrim Fathers called the early settlers?
Student: Because they paid their bills on time?

What are the two good things about being a teacher?
July and August.

Why was the principal worried?
Because there were so many rulers in the school.

Teacher: What did it say on the door of the pharaoh's tomb?
Student: Toot 'n' come in.

Why did the teacher turn on the lights?
Because her students were so dim.

Jasmine: I wish I'd lived a long time ago.
Teacher: Why?
Jasmine: Then I'd have less history to learn.

Mr. Hancock: Who can tell me what people from Scotland mean by "lads and lasses"?

Xavier: I know—lads are boys, and lassies are dogs!

Teacher: If you had five candy bars and your little brother asked you for one, how many would you have left?

Student: Five, of course!

Why can't executioners learn French?

Because they know no merci.

Principal at an assembly: Last night someone broke into the school supply room and stole a bunch of blunt pencils. The police described the theft as pointless.

Why did the boy take a ladder to school?
Because it was a high school.

Max: Why are you sitting in the gerbil's cage?
Joshua: Because I want to be the teacher's pet!

Why do principals never look out of the window in the mornings?
Because they wouldn't have anything to do in the afternoons.

What do you call someone who keeps on talking when no one is listening?
A teacher!

Teacher: Why do birds fly south in the winter?
Student: Because it's too far to walk.

Teacher: Carlos, don't hum while you're working.
Carlos: I'm not working— I'm just humming.

Teacher: Where are you from?
Student: America.
Teacher: Which part?
Student: All of me!

Teacher: What's 5q plus 5q?
Yoko: 10q.
Teacher: You're welcome!

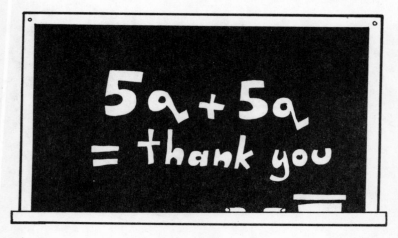

Why did the children eat candy in class?

Because their teacher told them not to.

Teacher: If I had five apples in one hand and six in another, what would I have?

Student: Big hands.

What's the best thing about going to school?
Coming home again.

BBBRRiiiNNG!!

Teacher: You've got your shoes on the wrong feet.
Small boy: These are the only feet I've got.

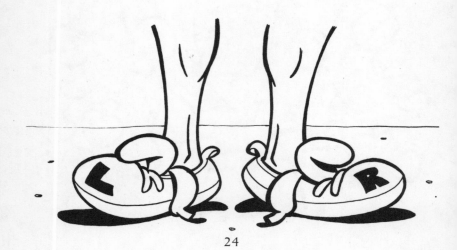

During the school Christmas play the three wise men came onto the stage. The first wise man put an envelope down in front of the crib. "Leo!" said the teacher. "You are supposed to give the baby Jesus gold!" "Yes," said Leo, "but this is a New York Yankees season ticket—my dad says they are as good as gold!"

What tools do we use in arithmetic?
Multipliers!

Teacher: Sarah, what's 12 times 12?

Sarah: 144.

Teacher: Good.

Sarah: Good? It's perfect!

Teacher: If I bought 100 cookies for 10¢, what would each cookie be?

Student: Stale.

What kind of tree does a math teacher climb?
A geometry.

Teacher: You have a nice voice, Jason, but please don't spoil it by singing!

There was once a very intelligent boy. Whenever he got a good report card, his father would give him 20¢ and a pat on the head. By the time he was 12 he had $500 and a very flat head.

Teacher: What's your favorite song?
Student: I have five: "Three Blind Mice" and "Tea for Two."

Robert: Sarah, you're stupid!

Sarah: Boo hoo . . . sob . . . sniff.

Teacher: Robert, that was very mean, say you're sorry right now.

Robert: Sorry you're stupid, Sarah.

Math teacher: Oscar, how many times have I told you to stop playing with that calculator?

Oscar: Er . . . 6,340 times!

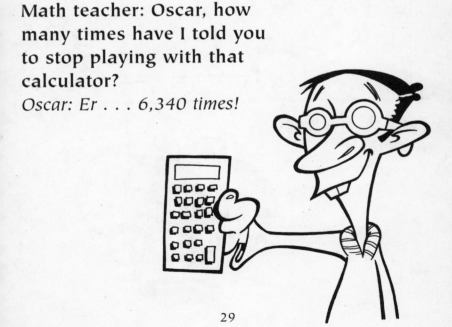

My teacher brought a math
plant to school this morning.
What do you mean?
She said it had square roots.

Why did the boy take
his car to school?
*To drive his teacher up
the wall.*

How do bees get
to school?
By school buzz!

Teacher: What do you
call the outside of a tree?
Boy: I don't know.
Teacher: Bark.
Boy: Woof!

Chemistry teacher: What are
nitrates?
*Student: I don't know, but I think
that they're better than day rates.*

Why did the teacher wear sunglasses?
Because her students were so bright.

Gym teacher: There are only two things stopping you from becoming the greatest athlete in the world, David.
David: What are they?
Gym teacher: Your feet, dear!

Teacher: What's the most important thing to remember in a chemistry lesson?
Student: Don't lick the spoon.

What do you call two people who embarrass you at Open House?
Mom and Dad!

No!

Mother: Why are you home from school so early, Tom?

Tom: Because I was the only one who could answer a tricky question.

Mother: Oh, really? What was the question?

Tom: Who threw the pencil at the principal?

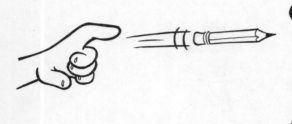

Teacher: How would you spell "amphibian"?

Student: I wouldn't—I would spell "frog."

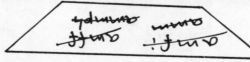

Little Sally, a first grade student, told her mom that she had broken off her engagement with her friend Carlo.
"Oh dear, why?" said her mom.
"Well," cried Sally, "I don't think he was ready for me, *and* he scribbled in my coloring book!"

"Mommy, the other children at school keep calling me a big head."
"Don't worry, sweetheart, there's nothing in it."

Dad: How are your grades at school?

Son: They're underwater.

Dad: What?

Son: They're below C!

"Is your hot lunch spicy?"

"No, smoke always comes out of my ears."

"I won a prize at school today, Mommy,"
said Emily. "Miss Trubsham asked how
many legs an elephant has, and I said,
"Three."
"Three?" said Mom. "Then how did
you win the prize?"
"I was closest," said Emily.

Why did the cell cross the microscope?
To get to the other slide.

Teacher: Who invented fractions?
Student: Henry the Eighth.

Teacher: For all those who were late this morning because they stayed up to watch the Super Bowl, we're going to make the school more like a football game.

Students: Hooray!

Teacher: So you can all stay behind and do extra time tonight as a penalty.

Students: Boo!

What's the worst thing you're likely to find in the school cafeteria?

The food.

Teacher: Why did knights in armor practice a lot?
Student: To stop them from getting rusty.

What do you call the small rivers that run into the Nile?
Juveniles.

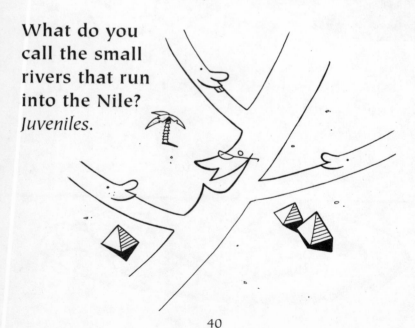

Math teacher: If you add 3,984 and 8,283, divide by three, and multiply by four, what do you get?
Student: The wrong answer!

What kind of food do math teachers eat?
Square meals.

"*Excuse me, there was a frog in Donna's burger.*"
"**Well, can't Donna speak for herself?**"
"*No, she's got the frog in her throat now!*"

Why were the naughty eggs sent out of class?
Because they kept playing practical yolks.

Teacher: Sam, why were you late for school this morning?

Sam: Well, the alarm was set for seven, but there are eight in our family.

What's the difference between school lunches and dog food?

School lunches come on plates.

Teacher: Sadie, why are you crawling to school ten minutes late?
Sadie: Because you told me never to walk in late again.

Teacher: I hope I didn't see you looking at Fred's test paper.
Student: I hope you didn't either!

How many rotten eggs
did the school cook put
into the omelettes?
A phew.

Teacher: Why were you late for school,
Jacob?
Jacob: I was stopping a fight between two boys.
Teacher: Excellent. How did you stop them?
Jacob: I kicked them both!

Get in the Saddle E. Z. Rider

Small Computers P. C. Jr.

Abracadabra Wiz Ard

Parachuting Hugo First

Sweeping Beauty I. M. A. Cleaner

Outside the Principal's Office Watts E. Dunn

School Lunches Buster Gutt

Rapping Made Easy *M. E. Nem*

Stop the Bus Isa Coming

Making Friends I. Malone

The Hurricane Rufus Blownoff

When Will We Meet Again?   Miles Apart

The Arctic Ocean   I. C. Waters

The Policeman's Rule Book   Laura Norder

A Load of Garbage   Stefan Nonsense

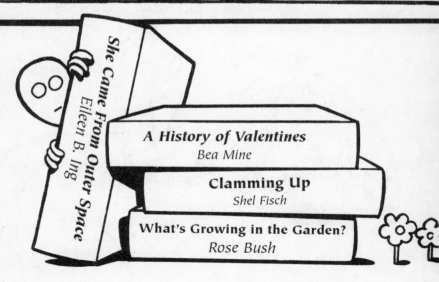

She Came From Outer Space   Eileen B. Ing

A History of Valentines
Bea Mine

Clamming Up
Shel Fisch

What's Growing in the Garden?
Rose Bush

Student: I thought we had a choice for lunch, but there's only salad.
School cook: That's the choice—take it or leave it!

Angry teacher: Didn't you hear me call you?
Student: But you told me not to answer back!

Teacher: Why are you always late for school, Jane?
Jane: Because you keep ringing the bell before I get here.

School cook: Eat your greens—they're good for your skin.
Student: But I don't want green skin!

Yuck!

Dad: Do you want some help with your homework, Danny?
Danny: No, thanks, Dad, I'll get it wrong on my own.

Student 1, outside cafeteria: Oh good, we're having salad today.
Student 2: How do you know it's salad?
Student 1: Well, I can't smell anything burning.

Art teacher: I asked you to draw a picture of a cow eating grass. Why have you handed in a blank piece of paper?

Student: Because the cow ate all of the grass, so there's no grass to draw anymore.

Art teacher: But where is the cow?

Student: Why should the cow hang around if there's no grass to eat?

Teacher: Your homework story "My Dog" is exactly the same, word for word, as your brother's.
Student: I know—it's the same dog.

Teacher: Maria, you've been doing Sam's homework again. I recognize your writing in his notebook.
Maria: No, I haven't. It's just that we both used the same pencil.

Teacher: How do you like doing your homework?
Student: I like doing nothing better!

Emily: Dad, I'm tired of doing my homework.
Dad: Come on, homework never killed anyone.
Emily: I know, but I don't want to be the first.

Student: Would you punish me for something I didn't do?
Teacher: Of course not.
Student: Good, because I haven't done my homework.

Madison: Why have you got a hot dog behind your ear?
Mr. James: Oh no, I must have eaten my pencil for lunch!

Music teacher: Why did you put that vegetable on the piano?
Student: You said my playing would improve if I had a beet!

A vampire's report card:
English: Good.
Math: Good.
Baseball: Shows promise as a bat.

Teacher: Give me a sentence with "I" in it.

Student: I is . . .

Teacher: No, you should always say "I am . . ."

Student: I am the ninth letter of the alphabet!

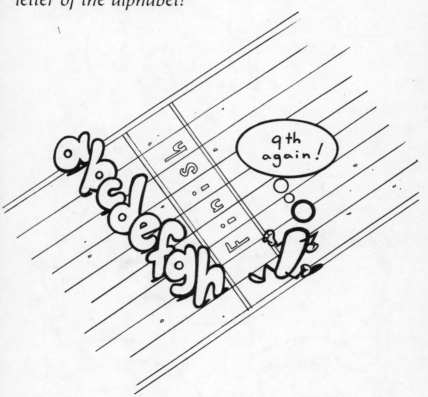

"Your report card is terrible, Fred," said his father. "And what's even worse is that it says you're very careless about your appearance."
"Really, Dad?"
"Yes, it says you haven't appeared in school for three weeks."

Teacher: Write the longest sentence you can.
Student: Easy! "Life imprisonment."

Geography teacher: If you were in the mid-Atlantic Ocean facing south, what would be on your right hand?
Student: Four fingers and a thumb.

English teacher: How do you spell "banana"?

Student: I'm not sure.

English teacher: Oh come on, it's easy: "B, a . . ."

Student: Yes, I know how to start, but I just don't know when to stop!

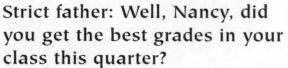

Strict father: Well, Nancy, did you get the best grades in your class this quarter?

Nancy: No, Dad. Did you get the best salary in your office?

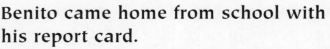

Benito came home from school with
his report card.

"Guess what, Dad. I've got some
great news for you."

His dad looked pleased. Benito said,
"You remember you promised me
$10 if I got a good report card?"

"Yes," said his father, reaching
for his wallet.

"You'll be happy to hear that
you don't have to pay me!"

Teacher: Give me a sentence with the word "centimeter" in it.
Student: My grandmother came to visit, and I was sent t' meet 'er at the bus station!

Teacher: Name two days of the week that begin with "T."
Student: Today and tomorrow.

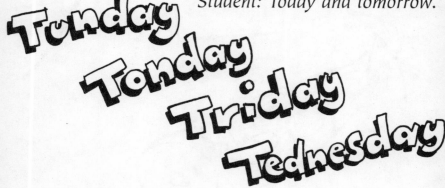

The sixth grade class was taking
a field trip on a boat. The principal was
reminding them about safety onboard.
*"Now then, what do you shout if a boy
falls overboard?"*
"Shout, 'Boy overboard!'" replied Michael.
*"Correct," said the principal. "And what if
a teacher falls overboard?"*
"Shout, 'Hooray!'" replied Michael.

Teacher: Can anyone
tell me the name of a
liquid that won't freeze?
Student: Hot water.